Report Writing: Removing the Stress!

REPORT WRITING: Removing the Stress!

By Silvia L. DeRuvo & Fred DeRuvo

Contents

3rd Grade:
- My Rain Forest 4
- My Native American Report 11

4th Grade:
- My Gold Rush 18
- My California Missions Report 30

5th Grade:
- My Colonial America Report 40
- My State Report 51

6th Grade:
- My Ancient Civilization Report 69
- My Country Report 85

Layout & Design: Fred DeRuvo

Published by Study-Grow-Know
PO Box 1592 • Hampton GA 30228

Find us on the 'Net:
http://www.adroitpublications.com • fred_deruvo@hotmail.com

Report Writing: Removing the Stress!
Notes to Parents/Teachers from the Authors

This book is the result of many hours of actual classroom instruction and learning. It has been thoroughly field-tested with Learning Handicapped and English Language Learners who lacked the organization skills to be proficient report writers.

What we have learned in this process is that *all* students have benefitted from this book of report writing templates. It has removed the fear and frustration for both students and parents and has provided the teacher in the classroom with another tool that can be utilized with all students, allowing them to become proficient, independent report writers.

Purpose:
The purpose of this book is to bridge the gap between graphic organizers and paragraph construction. Students often know how to develop graphic organizers based on a particular subject, but then have a difficult time putting those ideas into complete sentences or organized paragraphs.

Using this book will help students know what to look for in their research, being prompted by the questions on the reproducible pages, respond to those questions in complete sentences and ultimately produce complete paragraphs.

Usage:
Report Writing: Removing the Stress! is designed so that the teacher and/or home schooling parent may copy each page for each child in their classroom. This book is intended for use *after* direct instruction and study of the subject matter. Students will *not* be able to do this independently without prior knowledge of vocabulary and concepts.

Once students have a working knowledge of the subject matter, they can then answer each question in the report template(s) using complete sentences, which will then provide them with complete paragraphs when they are finished.

In this way, students are independently writing their report(s) without the direct intervention from the teacher or parent to produce the final result. Students will know and feel good about the fact that they have accomplished the report writing essentially *on their own*.

Report Writing: Removing the Stress!

Some images used in this publication were created by artists at New Vision Technologies and are copyright protected. Used with permission.

Images used in this publication (unless otherwise noted) are from clipartconnection.com and used with permission, ©2007 JUPITERIMAGES, and its licensors. All rights reserved.

Permission is granted to the individual purchaser, to reproduce each page of this book for classroom use only.

Originally published 2006 by Adroit Publications, Inc.

Report Writing: Removing the Stress!

My Rain Forest Report

By: _____

Date: _____

Class: _____

Report Writing: Removing the Stress!

My Rain Forest Report

Contents

What is a Rain Forest? .... Page _____

The Emergent Layer .... Page _____

Canopy .... Page _____

Understory .... Page _____

Forest Floor .... Page _____

Rainforest Gifts .... Page _____

Conclusion .... Page _____

Report Writing: Removing the Stress!

My Rain Forest Report

NAME: _____

SAMPLE QUESTION/ANSWER FORMAT

This teaches students to respond in *complete sentences,* including the question in
the answer.

1. What is a rain forest?
    Answer: *A rain forest is a forest that has very hot and wet weather all the time.*

2. How much rain does a tropical rain forest get in one year?
    Answer: *A tropical rain forest gets 240 inches of rain in one year.*

3. How many days of the year does it rain in a rain forest?
    Answer: *In a rain forest, there are about two hundred rainy days in one year.*

4. Where are the tropical rain forests found?
    Answer: *Tropical rain forests are found near the Equator.*

I. **The Rain Forest**

What is a rain forest?

_____

How much rain does a tropical rain forest get in one year?

_____

Report Writing: Removing the Stress!

How many days of the year are the rainy days in a rain forest?

_____

Where are the tropical rain forests found?

_____

II. The Emergent Layer

How tall are the trees in the Emergent Layer?

_____

Describe the trees in the Emergent Layer.

_____

What animals could be found in this layer?

_____

III. The Canopy

How tall are the trees in the Canopy?

_____

Why are these trees called the Canopy?

_____

What are some of the plants and foods that grow in the Canopy?

_____

What animals live in the Canopy?

_____

Name the four levels of the rain forest.

_____

_____

IV. The Understory

How tall are the trees in the Understory?

_____

Describe the different types of plants found in the Understory.

_____

Describe what it is like in the Understory.

_____

What kinds of animals and insects would be found in the Understory?

_____

V. The Forest Floor

What plants might grow on the Forest Floor?

_____

Why would there be just a few plants found on the Forest Floor?

_____

Describe what it is like on the Forest Floor?

_____
_____

What kinds of animals and insects live on the Forest Floor?

_____

VI. Rain Forest Gifts

Why is the rain forest important?

_____

How does the rain forest help us have clean air?

_____

What are some of the things that rain forests give us that we use every day?

_____

VII. Conclusion

What is one important thing you learned about the rain forest?

_____

Report Writing: Removing the Stress!

If you visited a rain forest, what plant or animal would you like to see? Why?

_____
_____

Why do you think it is important to save the rain forests?

_____
_____

Draw a picture of your favorite rain forest animal.

Report Writing: Removing the Stress!

My Native American Report

Name of My Tribe: _____

By: _____

Date: _____

Class: _____

Report Writing: Removing the Stress!

Contents

Tribe .... Page _____

Homes .... Page _____

Clothing .... Page _____

Food .... Page _____

Travel .... Page _____

Ceremonies .... Page _____

Art .... Page _____

Children .... Page _____

Report Writing: Removing the Stress!

My Native American Report

NAME: _____

I. Tribe

What is a tribe?
_____

What is the name of the tribe that this report is about?
_____

What does this name mean?
_____

In what part of the North America did your tribe live: Northwest, California Inter-Mountain, Southwest, East Woodlands, Plains, or Far North?
_____

In what state or states did your tribe live?
_____

II. Homes

What were their homes called?
_____

What things were used to build their homes?
_____

Describe what their homes looked like.

_____

_____

III. Clothing

What was your tribe's clothing made of: tree bark, deerskin, buffalo hide or something else?

_____

Describe the clothing of your tribe.

_____

_____

How was their clothing decorated?

_____

_____

IV. Food

Did your tribe hunt, fish, gather, or farm to get their food?

_____

_____

What were some of the tools or weapons they used to get food?

_____

_____

Describe some of the foods your tribe ate.

_____

_____

Draw a picture of one of the foods.

V. Travel

How did your tribe move from place to place?
_____

Describe what they used to travel in to get to other places.
_____

Why did your tribe travel from place to place?
_____

VI. Ceremonies

Does your tribe have any special ceremonies?
_____

Describe at least one special ceremony of your tribe.
_____

Why did your tribe perform this ceremony?
_____

Draw a picture of something they used in this ceremony.

VII. Art

Tell about some special art that your tribe made. This could be sand paintings, totem poles, masks, baskets, paintings on teepees, jewelry, or something else!

_____
_____

Why did they make this kind of art?

_____
_____

How did they learn how to make this art?

_____
_____

VIII. Children

What were some of the jobs of the children in your tribe?

_____
_____

Describe what you would do if you were a child in your tribe.

_____
_____

What are some of the games you might play?

_____

Report Writing: Removing the Stress!

My Gold Rush Report

My Gold Rush Report

By: _____

Date: _____

Class: _____

Report Writing: Removing the Stress!

Contents

Pioneers .... Page _____

Mexico Defeated .... Page _____

The Gold Rush .... Page _____

Routes to California .... Page _____

Gold Mining .... Page _____

Effect on California .... Page _____

Report Writing: Removing the Stress!

My Gold Rush Report

NAME: _____

I. Introduction

Paragraph 1: For this paragraph, you will answer the questions below using complete sentences about how the pioneers came to California to form settlements. When you have answered all the questions, rewrite them on a separate piece of paper in paragraph form.

Name three types of pioneers that came to California
_____
_____

What did each of the pioneers come to California to do?
_____
_____

Name at least one important California pioneer.
_____
_____

What did this famous pioneer do?
_____
_____

II. Mexico Defeated

Where and when did the Bear Flag Revolt take place?

_____

Who led the revolt and why?

_____

_____

What town did the rebels take over?

_____

_____

Why is it called "The Bear Flag Revolt"?

_____

_____

III. Taking California

When did the Mexican-American War begin?

_____

_____

Why did the United States decide to go to war with Mexico?

_____

_____

Where did most of the fighting in the war take place?

_____

_____

When and where did Mexico sign a treaty with the United States that ended in war?

_____

_____

Was California the only land that became part of the United States after the war? What states are in that area today?

_____

_____

IV. Discovering Gold

On what date was gold discovered in California and where?

_____

_____

Who discovered the gold and what was he doing when he discovered it?

_____

_____

With whom did Marshall share his discovery?

_____

_____

Were they able to keep their discovery a secret?

_____
_____

What happened when others found the gold at Sutter's Mill?

_____
_____

V. Getting to the Gold

What were the three routes that the gold miners took to California?

_____
_____
_____

Tell about the overland route: how long did it take to travel, what method of travel was used and what were the advantages, if any?

_____
_____
_____

Why did people choose this route?

_____
_____
_____
_____

Tell about some of the hardships people went through on this route.

_____
_____
_____

Why would you choose, or not choose, to take this route? Explain your answer.

_____
_____
_____

VI. The Sea Route

How long did it take, what method of travel was used and what were the advantages of this route?

_____
_____
_____

Why did people choose this route?

_____
_____

What were some of the hardships people went through on this route?

_____
_____
_____

Why would you choose or not choose this route?

_____

_____

VII. The Panama Route

How long did it take, what method of travel was used and what were the advantages of this route?

_____

_____

_____

Why did people choose this route?

_____

_____

What were some of the hardships people went through on this route?

_____

_____

_____

Why would you choose or not choose this route? Explain.

_____

_____

What route would you have chosen if you were a "Forty-Niner"? Why?

_____

_____

_____

VIII. Mining Methods

What did a miner have to do before he began mining in an area?

_____

_____

_____

_____

Name the three methods of mining that gold miners used.

_____

_____

_____

Explain the panning method.

_____

_____

_____

_____

Explain large scale mining methods.

_____
_____
_____
_____

IX. The Miner's Life

What kind of home did a miner live in?

_____
_____
_____
_____

Tell about the hardships that miners experienced.

_____
_____
_____

How did the hardships affect the miners?

_____
_____
_____
_____

Report Writing: Removing the Stress!

Do you think you would have liked being a miner? Why or why not?

_____

_____

X. Changing California

When miners were not successful, what did they do?

_____

_____

_____

_____

If they stayed in California, name some of the things they did.

_____

_____

_____

Did the Gold Rush bring people from other parts of the world to California?

_____

_____

_____

Do you think the Gold Rush was good or bad for California? Explain your answer.

_____

_____

_____

_____

Report Writing: Removing the Stress!

My California Mission Report

The Name of My Mission is: _____

By: _____

Date: _____

Class: _____

Report Writing: Removing the Stress!

My California Mission Report

TABLE of CONTENTS

Mission .... page _____

Location .... page _____

Description .... page _____

History of Mission .... page _____

Father Serra .... page _____

Purpose of the Mission .... page _____

Problems at the Mission .... page _____

Report Writing: Removing the Stress!

My California Mission Report

NAME: _____

I. Introduction

What is the name of the mission you are reporting on?
_____

Who is this mission named after?
_____
_____

When was this mission built?
_____

Who founded this mission?
_____
_____

Out of the 21 missions, what number is this mission?
_____
_____

II. Mission Location

Where is your mission located?
_____

What cities or towns are near the mission today?

_____
_____
_____

Along the El Camino Real, what missions could be found before and beyond this?

_____
_____
_____

Why was this a good location for this mission?

_____
_____

III. Describe Your Mission

What does this mission look like? Include number of buildings, shape of buildings, materials used in the building, shape of bell tower, etc.

_____
_____
_____

Report Writing: Removing the Stress!

What makes this mission different from the others?

_____

_____

_____

_____

How is the mission different today from when it was first built?

_____

_____

_____

What were some of the things that happened that changed the way your mission looks? Include any fires, earthquakes, or floods.

_____

_____

_____

When was this mission rebuilt or restored to look like it does today?

_____

_____

What is this mission used for today?

_____

_____

IV. History of California Missions

Who founded the missions in California?

_____
_____
_____
_____

Who sent Father Junipero Serra to California to found the missions?

_____
_____
_____

When was he sent to found the missions?

_____
_____
_____

Why was Father Serra sent to establish missions in California?

_____
_____

V. Father Serra

When and where was Father Serra born?

_____

How old was Father Serra when he began founding missions in California?

How many missions did he found in his life time?

How old was Father Serra when he died?

VI. Purpose of California Missions

What were the reasons Father Serra established the California Missions?

What did Father Serra offer the Indians?

_____
_____
_____

How did the Indians benefit from joining the California Missions?

_____
_____
_____

What did the Indians lose when they joined a mission? What did they get in return for the work that they did at the mission?

_____
_____

VII. Life on Your Mission

Who lived and worked on the missions?

_____
_____
_____
_____

What kind of jobs did they do?

_____
_____

Report Writing: Removing the Stress!

What were some of the animals and crops grown on your mission?

_____

_____

_____

Describe some of the daily activities at your mission.

_____

_____

VIII.   Problems at California Missions

Why were some of the Indians unhappy with their lives on the missions?

_____

_____

_____

_____

Why were the missions bad for some of the Indian people?

_____

_____

_____

Do you think that life on a mission really helped or hurt the Indians? Why?

_____

_____

IX. Conclusion

What did you learn about your mission from writing this report?

_____
_____
_____
_____

Would you visit this mission if you had the opportunity? Why or why not?

_____
_____
_____

What would you probably want to see if you visited this mission?

_____
_____
_____

Would you recommend visiting this mission to a friend? Why or why not?

_____
_____

Report Writing: Removing the Stress!

My New England Colonies Report

By: _____

Date: _____

Class: _____

Report Writing: Removing the Stress!

My New England Colonies Report

TABLE of CONTENTS

Introduction .... page _____

Puritan Community .... page _____

Puritans and the Land .... page _____

Life in New England .... page _____

Puritans and Education .... page _____

Puritan Family Life .... page _____

Religion and Government .... page _____

Problems with Puritan Society .... page _____

Conclusion .... page _____

Report Writing: Removing the Stress!

My New England Colonies Report

NAME: _____

I. Introduction

Who were the Puritan Colonists?
_____
_____

The Puritan Colonists were citizens of what country?
_____
_____

Why did they come to New England?
_____
_____
_____

What did the Puritans object to in the traditional English churches?
_____
_____

What did they believe should be their first concern in life?
_____
_____
_____

What did they believe would happen to them if they disobeyed God?

_____

II. Puritan Community

Where did the Puritans settle in New England?

_____

_____

Describe a Puritan town. Include the various buildings and plots of land.

_____

_____

What did a typical family plot of land have on it?

_____

_____

How were animals kept away from the crops growing in the fields?

_____

_____

III. Puritans and the Land

Had the Puritans made a good choice in settling in Massachusetts? Explain.

_____

_____

Why was farming difficult for the Puritans?

_____
_____
_____

What did some Puritans do since farming was difficult?

_____
_____
_____

IV. Life in New England

Describe some of the expectations of Puritan children.

_____
_____
_____

Why were Puritan parents so strict?

_____
_____
_____

What did Puritan parents feel they had to guard against?

_____
_____
_____

Why were children often sent away to live with relatives at the age of 13?

What were some of the skills they learned while they were apprentices?

V. Puritans and Education

Why was learning to read so important to the puritans?

Did all Puritan children attend school or were some schooled at home?

Was schooling as important for girls as it was for boys?

_____
_____
_____

Why was Harvard College founded by Puritans?

_____
_____

VI. Puritan Family Life

Why did Puritans have large families?

_____
_____
_____
_____

Describe a Puritan home. Include the house and furniture inside.

_____
_____
_____

How did the puritans pass on their way of life from generation to generation?

_____
_____

What did the fathers teach their sons?

_____

_____

What did the mothers teach their daughters?

_____

_____

What did young men do at the age of 23?

_____

_____

How did sons get their own land?

_____

_____

VII. Puritan Religion and Government

In the Puritan Colonies, were government and religion kept separate? Give an example.

_____

_____

_____

_____

Report Writing: Removing the Stress!

What did the Puritans believe about democracy? Why?

_____
_____
_____

Who could vote in a Puritan society?

_____
_____
_____

Would could be chosen to be a leader?

_____
_____

Did the Puritans allow any other religious freedom?

_____
_____

What did Puritans do to those people who believe in other religions?

_____
_____
_____

VIII. Problems with the Puritan Society

Who was a dissenter?

_____
_____
_____
_____

Who did the Puritans consider to be dissenters?

_____
_____

What did some of the dissenters believe?

_____
_____
_____

What happened to people who were dissenters?

_____
_____

What colony did many of the dissenters escape to?

_____
_____

What were some of the other forms of punishment used on those who broke Puritan laws?

___

IX. Conclusion

In two or three sentences, describe daily life in Puritan New England.

___

Do you think you would prefer to live in a Puritan colony or in current times? Why?

___

If you could visit a New England Colony, what you would hope to see there?

___

My State Report

STATE: _____

By: _____

Date: _____

Class: _____

My State Report

TABLE of CONTENTS

Location .... page _____

History .... page _____

Physical Features .... page _____

Political Features .... page _____

State Flag .... page _____

State Bird .... page _____

State Flower .... page _____

Climate .... page _____

Points of Interest .... page _____

Government .... page _____

Economy .... page _____

Conclusion .... page _____

Bibliography .... page _____

I. Location of Your State

In which part of the United States is your state locate?

_____
_____

What is the area of your state in square miles?

_____
_____
_____

What other states and/or bodies of water border your state?

_____
_____
_____

How many miles is it from the northernmost border to the southernmost?

_____
_____
_____

How many miles is it from the eastern border to the western border?

_____
_____

II. History of Your State

When was your state admitted to the United States?

_____
_____
_____

Prior to being admitted, who settled in your state?

_____
_____

Why did those settlers come to your state?

_____
_____
_____

Describe a significant event in the history of your state.

_____
_____

III. Physical Features - Geography

What are the topographical regions in your state? (Include any mountain ranges, plateaus, plains, valleys, peninsulas, gulfs, deserts, or islands.

_____

Report Writing: Removing the Stress!

_____

_____

_____

What are the important rivers and lakes in your state?

_____

_____

_____

What are the highest and the lowest points in your state?

_____

_____

_____

What is the most outstanding geographical feature of your state?

_____

_____

IV. Political Divisions of Your State

Where is your state capital?

_____

_____

_____

_____

What are the largest cities in your state?

_____

_____

What is the population of your state?

_____

_____

How is your state ranked in population density?

_____

_____

What is the average population density of your state?

_____

_____

V. State Flag

What does the flag of your state look like?

_____

_____

What do the colors on your flag mean?

_____

_____

What symbols are on the flag? What do these symbols mean?

_____

_____

_____

When was the flag of your state adopted?

_____

_____

Illustrate your flag in the space below.

VI. State Seal

What does your state seal look like?

_____
_____
_____
_____

Describe the symbols on your state seal.

_____
_____
_____

Why were these symbols chosen and used?

_____
_____

Illustrate your state seal in the space below.

VII. State Bird

What kind of bird is your state bird?

_____
_____
_____
_____

Describe what your state's bird looks like.

_____
_____
_____

Why was that bird chosen as the state bird?

_____
_____
_____

Draw your state bird.

VIII.   State Flower

What is your state flower?

_____
_____

Describe your state flower.

_____
_____
_____

Why was this flower chosen as the state flower?

_____
_____
_____

Draw your state flower.

IX. Climate

What is the overall climate of your state like?

_____
_____
_____

What is the average temperature during the coldest months?

_____
_____

What is the average temperature during the hottest months?

_____
_____
_____

What is the average winter like in your state?

_____
_____
_____

What is the average summer like in your state?

_____
_____

What is the average rainfall/snowfall in your state in one year?

___

X. National Parks

Name at least one national or state park in your state.

___

Where is the park located?

___

What are some of the things you might see and do there?

___

Name at least one historical site located in your state and what would you see there?

___

Name at least one other point of interest in your state.

_____

_____

Why is that a point of interest?

_____

_____

What would you see at this point of interest?

_____

_____

XI. Government

What is the name of your state's capital?

_____

_____

Who is the current governor of your state?

_____

_____

_____

Which political party does he/she represent?

_____

How many senators and assembly members represent your state in Congress?

_____

_____

How many senators and representatives represent your state legislature?

_____

_____

How is your local government divided? How many divisions are there?

_____

_____

_____

XII. Economy

What are the agricultural resources of your state?

_____

_____

_____

Explain some of the different types of crops grown. Do farmers raise livestock as well?

_____

_____
_____

What are the forestry and/or fishing resources of your state?

_____
_____
_____

What are the mineral resources of your state?

_____
_____

What are the manufacturing resources of your state?

_____
_____

What are the energy resources of your state?

_____
_____

Does your state have any other resources?

_____
_____

XIII. Conclusion

Why would you, or would you not want to live in this state?

_____
_____
_____
_____

If you visited your state, describe at least two things you would see or do while there.

_____
_____
_____

Tell at least three things you learned about your state from writing this report

_____
_____
_____

XIV. Extra Credit

Find a song or poem written about your state. Write the words to the song or poem and don't forget to include the author's name. (Use a separate piece of paper if necessary.)

_____
_____

Tell about two famous people from your state.

_____

Report Writing: Removing the Stress!

_____
_____

What are some recreational activities you might enjoy in your state?

_____
_____
_____

Write about the wildlife in your state.

_____
_____
_____

Write about some of the plants that are native to your state.

_____
_____
_____

Tell about several colleges and universities and where they are located in your state.

_____
_____
_____

Tell about some of your state's cultural institutions (like museums) and what you would see if you visited them.

_____

_____

Describe the ethnic diversity in your state. What nationalities are represented in your state?

_____

_____

_____

Report Writing: Removing the Stress!

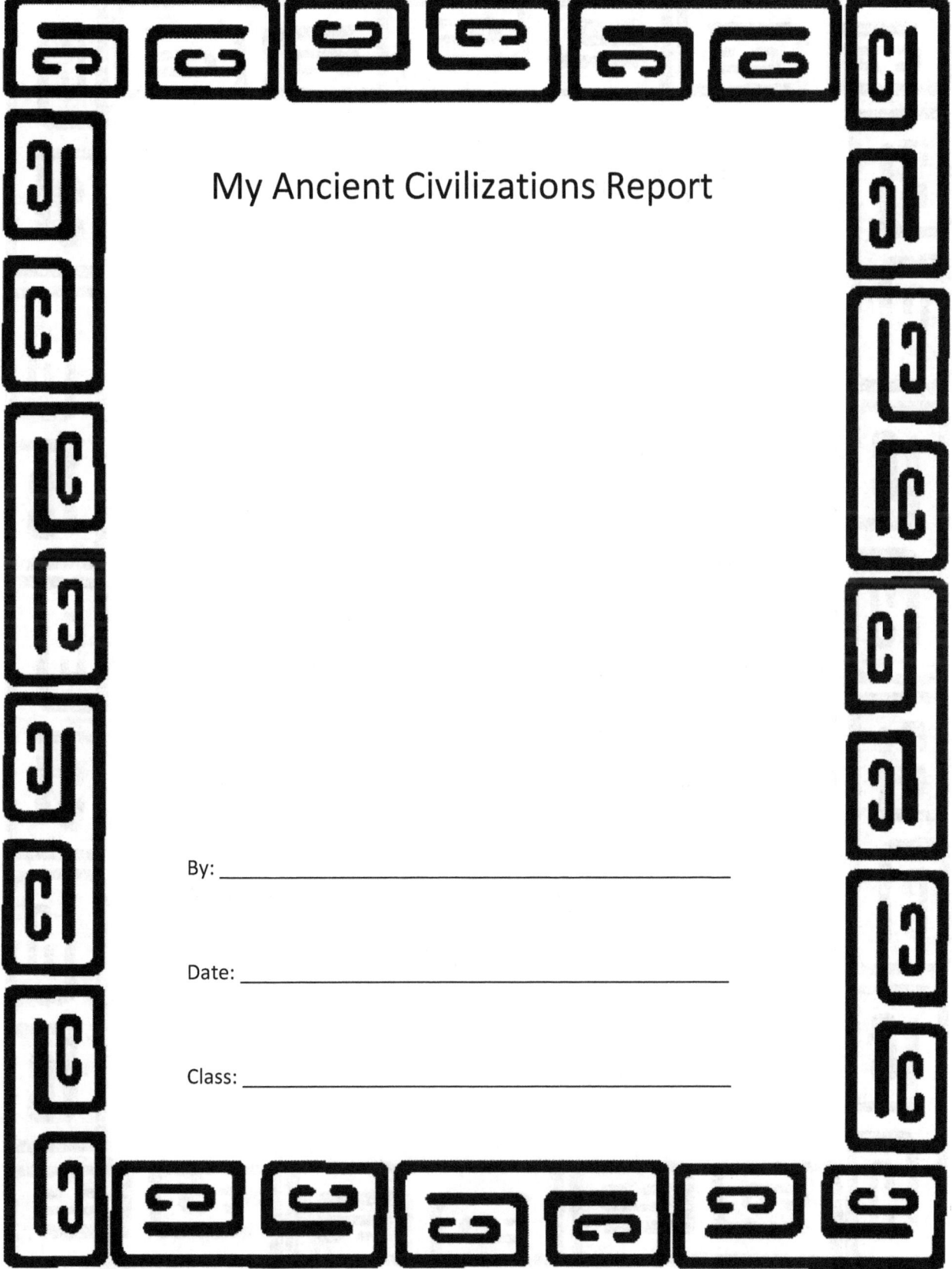

My Ancient Civilizations Report

By: _____

Date: _____

Class: _____

Report Writing: Removing the Stress!

My Ancient Civilizations Report

TABLE of CONTENTS

What's in a Name? .... page ____

Location .... page ____

Geography .... page ____

Political Features .... page ____

Climate .... page ____

Money .... page ____

Government .... page ____

Education .... page ____

Population .... page ____

Economy .... page ____

Conclusion .... page ____

Bibliography .... page ____

Report Writing: Removing the Stress!

I. What's in a Name?

What is the ancient civilization your report is about?

_____
_____

Who began this ancient civilization?

_____
_____
_____

Where did these people migrate from?

_____
_____
_____

How did this ancient civilization get its name?

_____
_____
_____

When did this civilization start?

_____
_____

Report Writing: Removing the Stress!

Why did you choose this ancient civilization for your report?

_____

_____

II. Location

On which continent is your civilization located?

_____

_____

_____

What is the distance from your ancient civilization's borders from the north to the south and from the east to the west?

_____

_____

What other civilizations or bodies of water are right next to your civilization?

_____

_____

_____

Explain the location of your civilization in relationship to the United States using directional
terms (N.S.E.W.)

_____

_____

III. Physical Features - Geography

What are the topographical regions in your civilization? (Include any mountain ranges, plateaus, plains, valleys, peninsulas, gulfs, deserts, or islands.

_____
_____
_____
_____

What are the important rivers and lakes in your civilization?

_____
_____
_____

What are the highest mountain and the lowest points in your civilization?

_____
_____
_____
_____

What is the most outstanding geographical feature of your civilization?

_____
_____
_____

IV. Political Divisions of Your State

How is your civilization divided into smaller political regions?

_____
_____
_____
_____

How is each political region governed?

_____
_____

What are the largest cities in your civilization?

_____
_____

V. Climate

What is the overall climate of your civilization like?

_____
_____
_____

What is the average temperature during the coldest months?

_____
_____

Report Writing: Removing the Stress!

What is the average temperature during the hottest months?

___

___

___

What is the average winter like in your civilization? How long does it last?

___

___

What is the average summer like in your civilization? How long does it last?

___

___

What is the average rainfall/snowfall in your civilization in one year?

___

___

How does your civilization's climate differ from the climate where you live?

___

___

VI. Money

What is the money of your civilization called?

_____
_____
_____

Are there different coins in your civilization? What are these coins called?

_____
_____

Describe the money in your civilization. Is it paper or coins, or both? What are the symbols
on the paper coins?

_____
_____

What is the value of your civilization's money compared to the United States?

_____
_____

Illustrate either a coin or piece of paper currency from your civilization.

VII. Government

What type of government does your civilization have?

_____
_____
_____

What are the different branches of government?

_____
_____

How are governmental decisions made?

_____
_____
_____

What is the leader of the government in your civilization called?

_____
_____

How is the leader chosen?

_____
_____

How is your civilization's government the same or different from ours?

_____

_____

VIII.   Education

At what ages do children in your civilization attend school?

_____

_____

_____

Are children in your civilization required to go to school?

_____

_____

Does it cost money to go to school or is it free? Explain.

_____

_____

_____

Do they have different levels of school and what are those levels?

_____

_____

Report Writing: Removing the Stress!

Do all children attend the same type of school or do some attend vocational schools?

_____

_____

What options do students have for college?

_____

_____

How is your civilization's educational system different from ours?

_____

_____

How are the schools the same as ours?

_____

_____

In what country would you like to attend school and why?

_____

_____

IX. Population

What is the overall population (in number amount) of your civilization?

_____
_____
_____

What is the population of your civilization's largest city?

_____
_____

How dense is the population of your civilization?

_____
_____
_____

What ethnic nationalities make up the population of your civilization?

_____
_____

Has there been a recent increase or decrease in population? If so, why?

_____
_____

Compare the population of your civilization to the population of the United States.

_____

_____

X. Economy

What are the three or four major resources of your ancient civilization?

_____

_____

_____

What are the agricultural resources of your civilization?

_____

_____

What are the forestry or fishing resources of your civilization?

_____

_____

_____

What are the mineral resources of your civilization?

_____

_____

What are the manufacturing resources of your civilization?

_____

_____

What are the energy resources of your civilization?

_____

_____

Are there any other economic resources of your civilization?

_____

_____

What type of jobs do most people have in your civilization?

_____

_____

XI. Conclusion

Why would you, or would you not want to live in this ancient civilization?

_____

_____

_____

Report Writing: Removing the Stress!

If you visited your civilization, describe at least three things you would see or do while you were there.

_____

_____

List at least three things that you learned about your civilization from writing this report.

_____

_____

_____

XII. Extra Credit

Draw and explain your ancient civilization's deities (if they have any).

_____

_____

_____

Describe at least three historical sites or points of interest in your civilization.

_____

_____

Describe at least three customs native to your civilization.

_____

_____

_____

What are some of the recreational activities of your civilization?

_____

_____

What are some of the ethnic foods from your ancient civilization?

_____

_____

Discuss whether or not your ancient civilization still exists today and if so, in what form?

_____

_____

Report Writing: Removing the Stress!

My Country Report

By: _____

Date: _____

Class: _____

Report Writing: Removing the Stress!

My Country Report

TABLE of CONTENTS

What's in a Name? ....page _____

Location ....page _____

Geography ....page _____

Political Features ....page _____

Flag..page _____

Climate ....page _____

Money ....page _____

Government ....page _____

Education ....page _____

Population ....page _____

Economy...page _____

Conclusion ....page _____

Bibliography ....page _____

Report Writing: Removing the Stress!

I. What's in a Name?

What is the country your report is about?

_____
_____

Who began this country?

_____
_____
_____

Where did these people migrate from?

_____
_____
_____

How did this country get its name?

_____
_____
_____

When did this country start?

_____
_____

Report Writing: Removing the Stress!

Why did you choose this country for your report?

_____

_____

II. Location

On which continent is your country located?

_____

_____

_____

What is the distance from your country's borders from the north to the south and from the east to the west?

_____

_____

What other countries or bodies of water border your country?

_____

_____

_____

Explain the location of your country in relationship to the United States using directional terms (N.S.E.W.)

_____

_____

III. Physical Features - Geography

What are the topographical regions in your country? (Include any mountain ranges, plateaus, plains, valleys, peninsulas, gulfs, deserts, or islands.

_____
_____
_____
_____

What are the important rivers and lakes in your country?

_____
_____
_____

What are the highest mountain and the lowest points in your country?

_____
_____
_____

What is the most outstanding geographical feature of your country?

_____
_____
_____

IV. Political Divisions of Your State

How is your country divided into smaller political regions?

_____
_____
_____
_____

How is each political region governed?

_____
_____

What are the largest cities in your country?

_____
_____

V. Flag

What does the flag of your country look like?

_____
_____

What do the colors on your flag represent?

_____
_____

What symbols are on the flag? What do these symbols mean?

_____

_____

Illustrate your country's flag here.

VI. Climate

What is the overall climate of your country like?

_____

_____

_____

What is the average temperature during the coldest months?

_____

_____

What is the average temperature during the hottest months?

_____
_____
_____

What is the average winter like in your country? How long does it last?

_____
_____

What is the average summer like in your country? How long does it last?

_____
_____

What is the average rainfall/snowfall in your country in one year?

_____
_____

How does your country's climate differ from the climate where you live?

_____
_____

VII. Money

What is the money of your country called?

_____
_____
_____

Are there different coins in your country? What are these coins called?

_____
_____

Describe the money in your country. Is it paper or coins, or both? What are the symbols on the paper coins?

_____
_____

What is the value of your country's money compared to the United States?

_____
_____

Illustrate either a coin or piece of paper currency from your country.

VIII. Government

What type of government does your country have?

_____
_____
_____

What are the different branches of government?

_____
_____

How are governmental decisions made?

_____
_____
_____

What is the leader of the government in your country called?

_____
_____

How is the leader chosen?

_____
_____

How is your country's government the same or different from ours?

_____

_____

IX. Education

At what ages do children in your country attend school?

_____

_____

_____

Are children in your country required to go to school?

_____

_____

Does it cost money to go to school or is it free? Explain.

_____

_____

_____

Are there different levels of schooling and what are those levels?

_____

_____

Report Writing: Removing the Stress!

Do all children attend the same type of school or do some attend vocational schools?

_____

_____

What options do students have for college?

_____

_____

How is your country's educational system different from ours?

_____

_____

How are the schools the same as ours?

_____

_____

In what country would you like to attend school and why?

_____

_____

X. Population

What is the overall population (in number amount) of your country?

_____
_____
_____

What is the population of your country's largest city?

_____
_____

How dense is the population of your country?

_____
_____
_____

What ethnic nationalities make up the population of your country?

_____
_____

Has there been a recent increase or decrease in population? If so, why?

_____
_____

Compare the population of your country to the population of the United States.

___

XI. Economy

What are the three or four major resources of your country?

___

What are the agricultural resources of your country?

___

What are the forestry or fishing resources of your country?

___

What are the mineral resources of your country?

___

What are the manufacturing resources of your country?

_____
_____

What are the energy resources of your country?

_____
_____

Are there any other economic resources of your country?

_____
_____

What type of jobs do most people have in your country?

_____
_____

XII. Conclusion

Why would you, or would you not want to live in this country?

_____
_____
_____

Report Writing: Removing the Stress!

If you visited your country, describe at least three things you would see or do while you were there.

_____

_____

List at least three things that you learned about your country from writing this report.

_____

_____

_____

XIII. Extra Credit

Draw and explain your ancient country's coat of arms.

_____

_____

_____

Write the words to your country's national anthem. (Use an extra piece of paper if necessary)

_____

_____

_____

Describe at least three historical sites or points of interest in your country.

_____

_____

Report Writing: Removing the Stress!

Describe at least three customs native to your country.

_____

_____

_____

Write about two or three famous people from your country.

_____

_____

_____

What are some of the recreational activities of your country?

_____

_____

What are some of the ethnic foods from your ancient country?

_____

_____

Discuss whether or not your country still exists today and if so, in what form?

_____

_____

Report Writing: Removing the Stress!

MONTH of _____ **Year** _____

Sunday	Monday	Tuesday	Wednesday	Thursday	Friday	Saturday

Sample Bibliography:

Examples:

- Taylor, Barbara, Rain Forest, Dorling Kinderslay Inc., 1992
- "Rain Forests," Microsoft Encarta, 1999 Encyclopedia, 1993-1999, Microsoft Corp.
- http://go.com/ (Search Engine used for finding information on the Internet)
- http://missions.bgmm.com/index.htm
- Getting to Know the Rain Forest, Carson Dellosa Publishing, 1993
- Armento, B. J., Nash, G. B. Salter, C. L. Wilcox, K. K. From Sea to Shining Sea, Boston.
  Houghton Mifflin Co., 1991. Unit Two "The Land and the First American," pp. 60-111
- Riddle, Patricia, Indian Unit, Mart, Inc., 1992
- California, Microsoft Encarta, 1999, Encyclopedia, California History, 1993-1999, Microsoft Corp.
- Grinsted, K., Countries of the World, Gareth Stevens Publishing. Milwaukee 1999
- Armento, B. J., Nash et al, America Will Be. Boston. Houghton Mifflin Co., 1991. Unit
  Three, Life in the English Colonies, Chapter 8, The New England Colonies, pp. 178-205

www.ingramcontent.com/pod-product-compliance
Lightning Source LLC
LaVergne TN
LVHW061216060426
835507LV00016B/1968